6-11

E   J
745.594   c.1
KEN
Kenney
Super simple jewelry

SUPER
SANDCASTLE™
Super Simple Crafts

SUPER SIMPLE
Jewelry

Fun and Easy-to-Make
Crafts for Kids

Karen Latchana Kenney

Consulting Editor, Diane Craig, M.A./Reading Specialist

ABDO
Publishing Company

Published by ABDO Publishing Company, 8000 West 78th Street, Edina, Minnesota 55439.
Copyright © 2010 by Abdo Consulting Group, Inc. International copyrights reserved in all countries. No part of this book may be reproduced in any form without written permission from the publisher. Super SandCastle™ is a trademark and logo of ABDO Publishing Company.

Printed in the United States of America, North Mankato, Minnesota.

Editor: Liz Salzmann
Content Developer: Nancy Tuminelly
Cover and Interior Design and Production: Oona Gaarder-Juntti, Mighty Media
Photo Credits: Colleen Dolphin, Shutterstock
Activity Production: Pam Scheunemann

The following manufacturers/names appearing in this book are trademarks:
Aleene's® Original Tacky Glue®, Plaid® Mod Podge®, Reynolds® Cut-Rite® Waxed Paper, Office Depot® Posterboard, Crayola® Washable Glitter Glue, Sculpey®, FIMO®, UHU® Stic

Library of Congress Cataloging-in-Publication Data

Kenney, Karen Latchana.
  Super simple jewelry : fun and easy-to-make crafts for kids / Karen Latchana Kenney.
     p. cm. -- (Super simple crafts)
  ISBN 978-1-60453-625-6
  1. Jewelry making--Juvenile literature. I. Title.

  TT212.K42 2010
  739.27--dc22
                                    2009000354
012010   032010

Super SandCastle™ books are created by a team of professional educators, reading specialists, and content developers around five essential components—phonemic awareness, phonics, vocabulary, text comprehension, and fluency—to assist young readers as they develop reading skills and strategies and increase their general knowledge. All books are written, reviewed, and leveled for guided reading, early reading intervention, and Accelerated Reader® programs for use in shared, guided, and independent reading and writing activities to support a balanced approach to literacy instruction.

Table of Contents

To Adult Helpers

Making the jewelry in this book is really simple. There are just a few things to remember to keep kids safe. Some of the projects need to be baked in an oven. Make sure to set rules about how to act around hot objects and the oven. Also, glue will be used in some activities. Make sure kids protect their clothes and work surfaces before starting.

Symbols

Look for these symbols in this book.

 Super Hot. Be careful! You will be working with something that is super hot. Ask an adult to help you.

 Adult Help. Get help! You will need help from an adult.

Jewelry You Create!

Do you want a new necklace or bracelet? You can make your own! It's simple to make jewelry. And super fun too! Use all kinds of supplies. Both recycled and new! Try some or all of the **projects** in this book. It's up to you! From start to finish, making super simple jewelry is fun to do!

Tools and Supplies

Here are many of the things you will need to do the **projects** in this book. You can find them online or at your local craft store.

seed beads

2- or 4-hole buttons

metal washers

Tacky Glue

Mod Podge

pony beads

felt

colorful paper

3D paint

leather cord

elastic cord

safety pins

scissors

pom poms

needle-nose pliers

glue stick

slotted screwdriver

cookie sheet

wax paper

paintbrushes

knitting needles

poster board

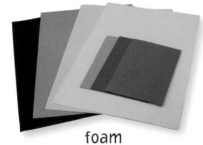
foam

glitter glue

polymer clay

masking tape

toothpicks

googly eyes

5

Fuzzy Critter Pins

Make cute critter pins for all your friends!

Supply List
- pom poms
- Tacky Glue
- googly eyes
- small foam pieces (optional)
- scissors
- poster board
- masking tape
- safety pins

1. Glue pom poms together to make your **critter**.

2. Glue on the googly eyes. You can also cut features out of foam.

3. Cut a piece of poster board for the back of the critter. Make sure it is a little bit smaller than your critter.

4. Put glue on one side of the poster board. Press your critter onto the poster board.

5. Carefully tape the safety pin to the back of your critter. Be sure to put the tape on the **clasp** side of the pin.

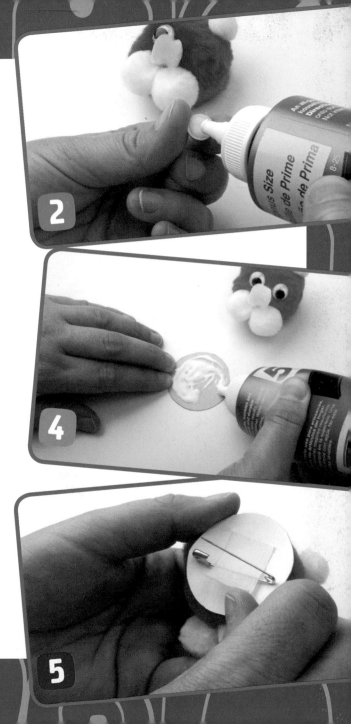

Button Bracelets

These colorful bracelets will use up all your extra buttons!

Supply List
- elastic cord
- scissors
- masking tape
- 2- or 4-hole buttons

1-2-3 Bracelet

1. Cut a piece of **elastic** cord that is 10 inches (25 cm) long. Put a piece of masking tape on one end.

2. Put buttons on the cord in a colorful pattern. Try using buttons that are different shapes and sizes.

3. Add enough buttons to go around your wrist. Then remove the tape. Hold on to the end so the buttons don't slide off! Tie the ends together with three tight knots. Cut off the extra cord.

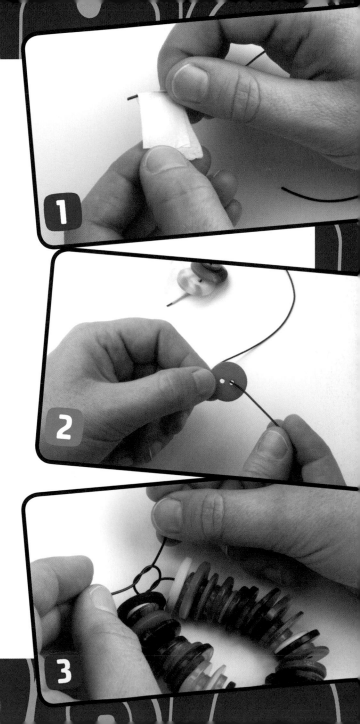

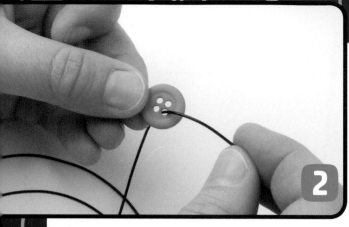

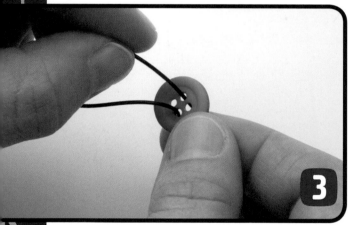

Button Up Bracelet

1 Cut a piece of **elastic** cord that is 10 inches (25 cm) long. Put a piece of tape 2 inches (5 cm) from one end.

2 Push the other end of the cord through a button. Go from back to front.

3 Push the cord back through the opposite hole in the button. Pull the button down to the tape.

4 Choose another button and **repeat** steps 2 and 3. Push the buttons together. The buttons will overlap.

5 Keep adding buttons in the same way. After a while see if it reaches around your wrist. If it doesn't, add more buttons.

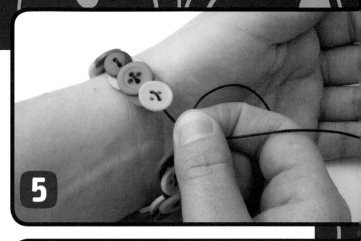

6 Finish with a big and a small button. Push the cord through the back of the big button. Then push it through the back of the small button.

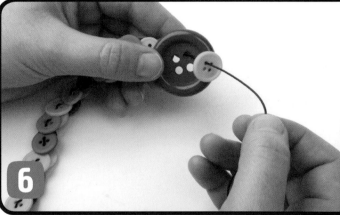

7 Push the cord back through both buttons. The small button should be in the middle of the large button.

8 Remove the tape and tie the ends of the cord together. Use three tight knots. Cut off the extra cord.

Safety Pin Jewelry

Shock your friends with cool jewelry made from safety pins!

Friendship Pin

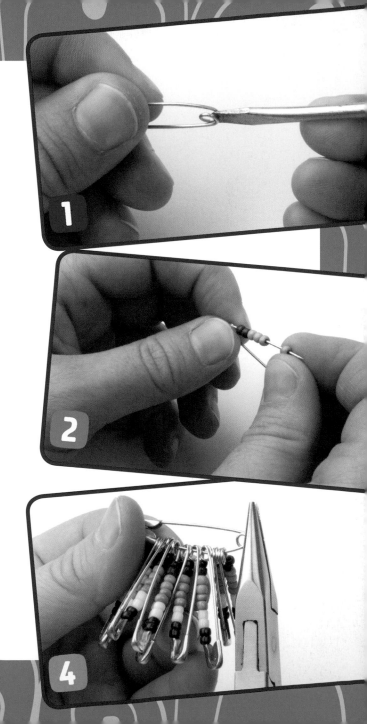

1. Choose a safety pin for the pin base. Use the screwdriver to spread open the pin's **coil** a little bit. Ask an adult to help you.

2. Now make some beaded pins to hang on the pin base. Open a pin and put seed beads on it. Use different colors and make a pattern. Add beads until the pin is full. Use a toothpick to put glue on the point of the pin. Then close the pin.

3. Make enough beaded pins to fill up the pin base. Put them on the pin base one at a time. Pull each beaded pin around the coil. They should hang from the **clasp** side of the base pin.

4. When the beaded pins are all on the base pin, use the pliers to squeeze the coil closed. Now your pin is ready to wear!

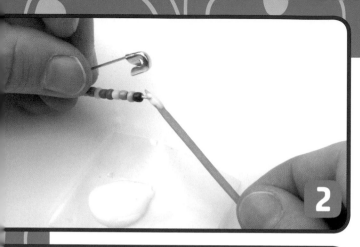

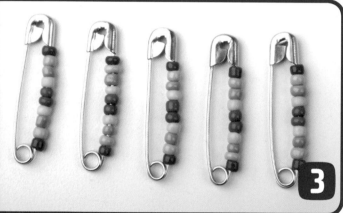

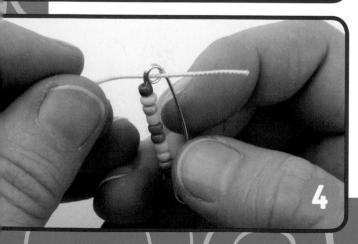

Pin Bracelet

1 Cut two pieces of **elastic** cord that are 10 inches (25 cm) long. Put a piece of masking tape on one end of each of the pieces of cord. Count out 30 to 40 safety pins. The pins should all be the same size. Put some glue on a piece of wax paper. Set out the beads.

2 Put the seed beads on the pins. Create colorful patterns. When each pin is full of beads, use a toothpick to add some glue to the point. Close the pin.

3 **Repeat** until you have made 30 to 40 beaded pins.

4 Push one of the cords through the **coil** of one of the pins. Put a bigger bead on the cord.

5 Push the cord through the **clasp** of another pin. Add another bigger bead.

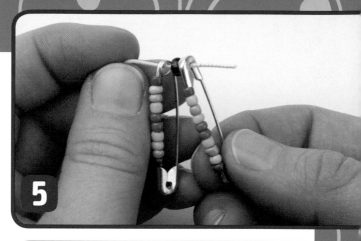

6 **Repeat** steps 4 and 5 until all of the pins are on the cord. Make sure the beaded sides of the pins all face the same way.

7 Lay the cord full of pins on the table. Push the second piece of cord through the other ends of the pins. Add a bead after each pin.

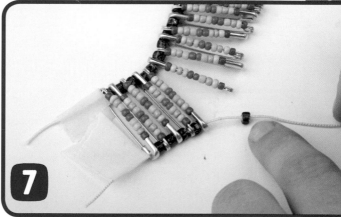

8 When all the pins are on both cords, you can check the length. Hold the cords on both sides and wrap the bracelet around your wrist. If it doesn't fit, add or take away pins until it's the right size for you.

9 Remove the tape. Tie the ends of each cord together. Use three tight knots on each cord. Put a dab of glue on the knots. Cut off the extra cord.

Fuzzy Felt Pins

Create your own colorful felt designs!

Supply List

- felt
  (in different colors)
- scissors
- Tacky Glue
- glitter glue
- 3D paint
- poster board
- safety pins
- masking tape

1. Cut the felt into some fun shapes. Glue them together.

2. Decorate your pin with glitter glue and 3D paint. Let it dry.

3. Cut a piece of poster board for the back of your pin. Make sure it is a little bit smaller than your **design**.

4. Glue the poster board to the back of your design.

5. Carefully tape a safety pin to the back of your design. Be sure to put the tape on the **clasp** side of the pin.

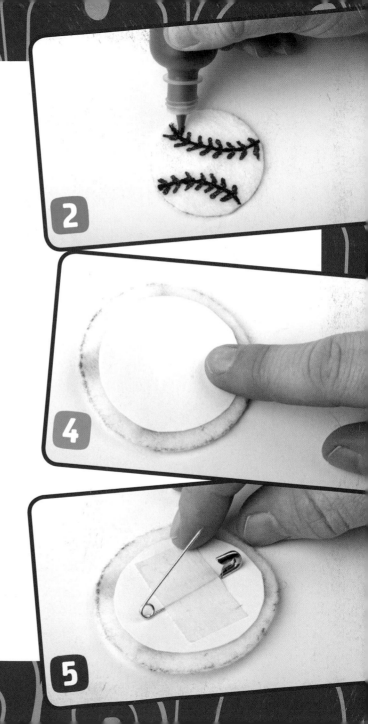

Paper Beads

Turn old paper scraps into a pretty new necklace!

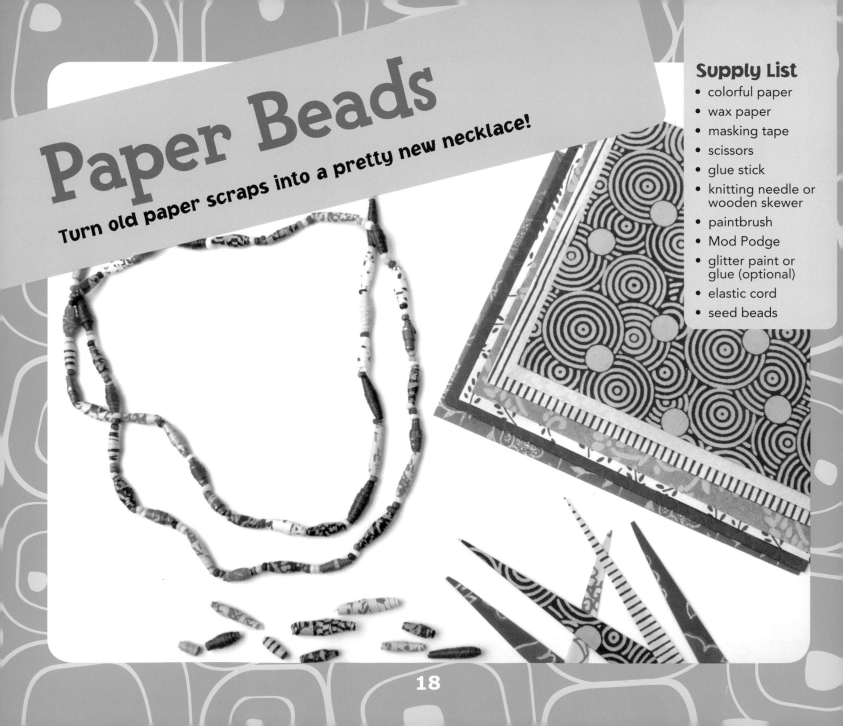

1. Find colorful pieces of paper to make your beads. Look in your paper recycling bin. Or ask an adult for leftover paper that you can use. Some examples are magazine or catalog pages, wrapping paper, **origami** paper, or any colored paper.

2. Spread out a large piece of wax paper. This will be your work surface. Use masking tape to hold down the edges.

3. Cut the paper into triangles. Try making them different sizes. The beads will be as wide as the bases of the triangles.

4. Lay a triangle out flat. Put the colored side down. Use a glue stick to put glue on the triangle. **Coat** the triangle from the middle to the point.

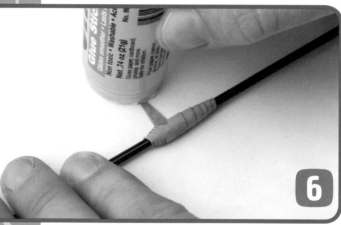

5 Roll the paper around a knitting needle or wooden **skewer**. Start at the bottom of the triangle.

6 Tightly roll the paper until you reach the tip. Make sure you keep the paper centered. Add more glue to help the point stick.

7 Gently slide the bead off of the knitting needle or wooden skewer. **Repeat** steps 4–7 until you have about 20 beads. Make more beads if you want a longer necklace.

8 Use a paintbrush to cover each bead with Mod Podge. Try not to get Mod Podge in the holes. Set the beads on wax paper to dry. After the Mod Podge dries you can add glitter paint or glitter glue.

9 Cut a piece of **elastic** cord that is about 25 inches (63 cm) long. Put masking tape on one end of the cord.

10 Put a paper bead on the cord. Then put three seed beads on the cord. Add another paper bead and three more seed beads.

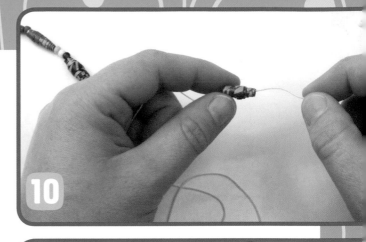

11 Keep adding paper beads and seed beads until your necklace is the length you want. Be sure there are at least 2 inches (5 cm) of cord left at the end.

12 Remove the tape. Tie the ends together with three tight knots. Cut off the extra cord.

Washer Wear

The latest in hardware fashion!

Supply List
- colorful paper
- metal washer
- pencil
- scissors
- Tacky Glue
- Mod Podge
- paintbrush
- leather cord
- pony bead

1. Choose a piece of colorful paper. Put a **washer** on the paper. Use a pencil to trace around the outside and inside circles of the washer.

2. Cut around the outside of the circle. Cut on the inside of the line. That way the line won't show on your necklace.

3. Gently fold the circle and make a small cut in the middle of the fold.

4. Unfold the circle. Cut out the center. Use the small cut you made as a starting place.

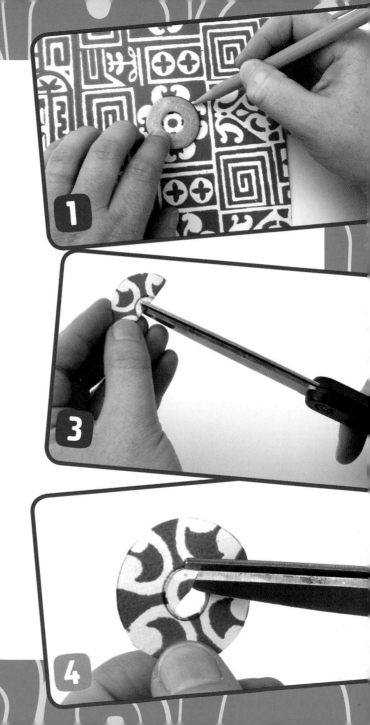

5 Glue the paper to the **washer**. Let the glue dry completely.

6 Use a scissors to cut off any edges of the paper that stick out.

7 Use something round, such as a pencil, to press in any extra paper into the center hole.

8 Paint the paper and the edges of the washer with Mod Podge. This will protect the paper. Let the Mod Podge dry completely.

9 Cut a 36-inch (91-cm) piece of leather cord. Fold it in half.

10 Put the fold through the center of the **washer**.

11 Wrap the ends of the cord around the washer. Put the ends through the fold. Pull the cord tight.

12 Put both ends of the cord through a pony bead. Push the pony bead against the washer. Tie a knot close to the pony bead.

13 Tie the ends of the cord together. Make sure the necklace fits over your head. Cut off the extra cord.

Funky Clay Beads

Twist, swirl, and shape clay to make these funky beads!

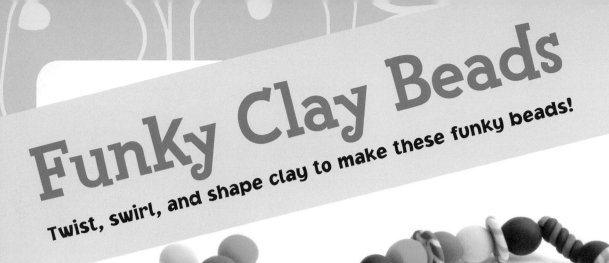

Basic Ball Beads

1. Take a piece of clay and squeeze it with your fingers. Keep squeezing until the clay is warm and soft.

2. Break off a small piece of the clay. Roll it into a ball.

3. Stick a toothpick through the middle of the ball. Twist the toothpick as you press it in to the ball. Pull the toothpick out of the bead.

4. Put wax paper on a cookie sheet. Place the finished bead on the wax paper.

5. **Repeat** steps 1–3 to make more beads. Bake the beads according to the clay manufacturer's directions.

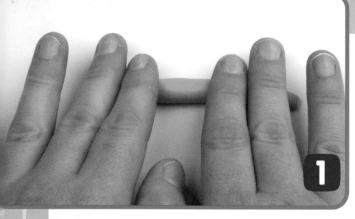

Twisty Beads

1 Break off a piece of warm, soft clay. Roll it into a rope.

2 Make another rope in a different color. The ropes should be the same size.

3 Wrap the ropes side by side around a toothpick. Make sure the ropes touch each other as you wrap them.

4 Gently twist the toothpick and pull it out of the clay.

5 Put wax paper on a cookie sheet. Place the finished bead on the wax paper.

6 **Repeat** steps 1–4 to make more beads. Bake the beads according to the clay manufacturer's directions.

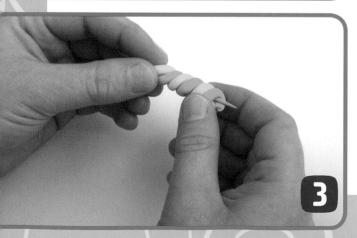

Peppermint Disk Beads

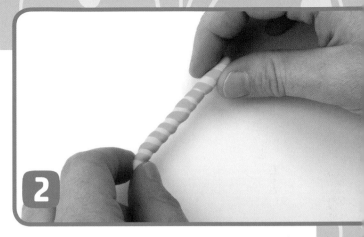

1. Break off a piece of warm, soft clay. Roll it into a rope. Make another rope in a different color.

2. Hold the ropes side by side. Twist them into a single rope. Twist more to make a smaller pattern.

3. Make a ball of clay the size of a pea. Press it flat into a disk shape.

4. Wrap the twisted rope around the disk. Break off any extra rope.

5. Smooth the **seam** where the rope touches the disk. Use a toothpick to make a hole in the center of the bead.

6. **Repeat** steps 1–5 to make more beads. Bake the beads according to the clay manufacturer's directions.

More Super Ideas

Swirly Beads

Mix two or more colors of clay to make a swirl. Don't mix too much or it will become one color! Then follow the basic ball bead steps on page 27.

Tube Beads

Make a short roll of clay. Wrap a thin rope of clay around the middle. The rope should be a different color. Stick a toothpick through the roll to make a hole.

Bumpy Beads

Add small dots of clay to a basic ball bead. Add the dots before removing the toothpick.

Stringing the Beads

1 Cut a piece of **elastic** cord. It should be 2 inches (5 cm) longer than you want the jewelry to be.

2 Put a piece of masking tape on one end. This keeps the beads from falling off the cord.

3 Start putting beads on the cord. You can try different patterns.

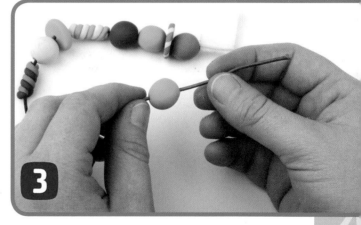

4 When you get close to the end, check the length. If it's a good fit, remove the tape and tie the ends together. Make three tight knots. Cut off the extra cord. If you can, tuck the knot into the hole of a bead.

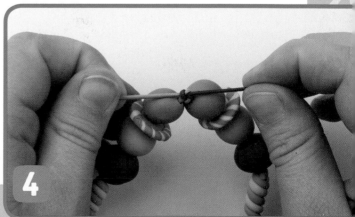

Glossary

clasp – the part that holds a pin, necklace, or bracelet closed.

coat – to cover completely with a substance such as paint or glue.

coil – a spiral or a series of loops.

critter – any animal.

design – a decorative pattern or arrangement.

elastic – able to be stretched.

origami – the Japanese art of folding paper into shapes.

project – a task or activity.

repeat – to do or say something again.

seam – the line where two edges meet.

skewer – a long, thin, wood, or metal stick with a sharp end.

washer – a flat ring made of metal, plastic, wood, or leather used to make something fit tightly.